HAL•LEONARD

INSTRUMENTAL
PLAY-ALONG

AUDIO
ACCESS
INCLUDED

PLAYBACK+
eed • Pitch • Balance • Loop

CLARINET

THE VERY

BACH

To access audio visit:
www.halleonard.com/mylibrary

Enter Code
4695-8128-4343-2638

ISBN 978-1-4950-9078-3

7777 W. BLUEMOUND RD. P.O. BOX 13819 MILWAUKEE, WI 53213

In Australia Contact:
Hal Leonard Australia Pty. Ltd.
4 Lentara Court
Cheltenham, Victoria, 3192 Australia
Email: ausadmin@halleonard.com.au

Visit Hal Leonard Online at
www.halleonard.com

ADAGIO
from OBOE CONCERTO IN F MINOR
BWV 1059

By JOHANN SEBASTIAN BACH

Clarinet

AIR

from ORCHESTRAL SUITE NO. 3
BWV 1068

By JOHANN SEBASTIAN BACH

Clarinet

Slowly and expressively

BIST DU BEI MIR

from NOTEBOOK FOR ANNA MAGDALENA BACH

BWV 508

CLARINET

By GOTTFRIED HEINRICH STÖLZEL

BOURRÉE IN E MINOR

from SUITE IN E MINOR FOR LUTE
BWV 996

Clarinet

By JOHANN SEBASTIAN BACH

INVENTION NO. 4
BWV 775

CLARINET

By JOHANN SEBASTIAN BACH

INVENTION NO. 14
BWV 785

Clarinet

By JOHANN SEBASTIAN BACH

JESU, JOY OF MAN'S DESIRING

from CANTATA 147
BWV 147

CLARINET

By JOHANN SEBASTIAN BACH

Moderately slow

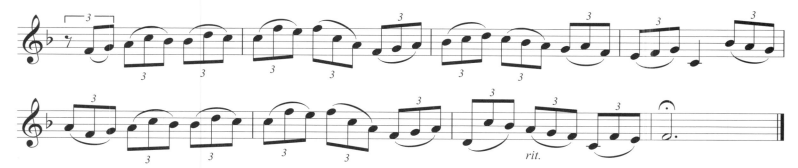

MINUET
from NOTEBOOK FOR ANNA MAGDALENA BACH
BWV Anh. 116

CLARINET

Composer Unknown

MINUET IN G MAJOR
from NOTEBOOK FOR ANNA MAGDALENA BACH
BWV Anh. 114

By CHRISTIAN PETZOLD

CLARINET

MINUET IN G MINOR

from NOTEBOOK FOR ANNA MAGDALENA BACH
BWV Anh. 115

Clarinet

By CHRISTIAN PETZOLD

MUSETTE
from NOTEBOOK FOR ANNA MAGDALENA BACH
BWV Anh. 126

CLARINET

Composer Unknown

POLONAISE IN G MINOR

from NOTEBOOK FOR ANNA MAGDALENA BACH
BWV Anh. 119

Clarinet

Composer Unknown

SHEEP MAY SAFELY GRAZE

from CANTATA 208
BWV 208

By JOHANN SEBASTIAN BACH

CLARINET

SICILIANO
from FLUTE SONATA IN E-FLAT MAJOR
BWV 1031

Clarinet

By JOHANN SEBASTIAN BACH

SLEEPERS, AWAKE
(Wachet Auf)
from CANTATA 140
BWV 140

By JOHANN SEBASTIAN BACH

CLARINET